MELANCHOLIA

poems

Wanda Deglane

"Wanda Deglane's "Melancholia", reminiscent of Wurtzel and Hornbacher, is a study in the heavy obligation of existence and the Sisyphean effort of surviving. This is an extremely poignant collection, full of prescriptions and blood ties, clutched steering wheels and the catharsis of screaming. It is an excellent and relatable read."

_**Kolleen Carney Hoepfner**, EIC of **Drunk Monkeys**, Author of *Your Hand has Fixed the Firmament* and *A Live Thing, Clinging with Many Teeth*

"Wanda Deglane's *Melancholia* is an ethereal eulogy to innocence detailed with emergency crayon candles, starfish in the sky for rocky road souls with marshmallows on fire who rely on texts from the pharmacist and 'the discreet paper bags' that, like Deglane's poetry, make 'living just a little more bearable.'"

_**Kristin Garth**, author of *Girlarium* and other books

"With *Melancholia*, Wanda Deglane strikingly and devastatingly collapses reality into a world punctuated by prescribed chemicals and ghosts that are not quite there. There is a compelling density to the knotty mass of *Melancholia* and as its matter assiduously becomes dislodged, its heaviness leaps from the book and despite all odds, floats above the reader as a haunting. There is much pleasure to be gleaned in how the poems seem to be subtle slanting rhymes for each other. This collection exquisitely wraps itself around unraveling and spiraling familial ties while staring clear-eyed at the resulting residual complex repercussions."

—**Bryon Cherry**, author of *Funeral Journey (Quail)*

"Both grounded and ethereal, this collection is equal parts dreamy and real. Wanda's poems feel intimate, like secrets being uttered to lovers, like activated photographs from a long-lost family album, like pill-kissed segments of pain, wisdom and observation. She gives commentary on mental health and our health care system in ways that are poignant and visceral; they will strike you right at your core."

—**Gina Tron**, *author of Suspect (Tarpaulin Sky)*

"Wanda Deglane's *Melancholia* is, to borrow a line of the poet's, 'ghostly and blooming.' Deglane renders the unspeakable moments of mental illness and family fractures into language so cutting and precise it will break your heart open. Let it. Come into this wondrous and haunting collection to find poems that bring the invisible to the surface, that blend nightmare and dreamscape, and that trace family longing and belongings and states of being into wonderment and wandering. Across safety pins, half-finished Mountain Dew, and antidepressants waiting at the pharmacy, this collection weaves a tapestry of what goes unspoken in mental illness while questioning a society that asks us, the mentally ill, not to be too loud, lest we disturb the peace we ourselves are not allowed. These poems shout back, even when they whisper. Deglane asks us to 'imagine the kind of desperation it must have taken to start / lighting everything around you on fire and hope it somehow saves you.' In doing so, we imagine this book: poems set on fire to stay alive and wow, what beauty we can gather from such light!"

—**Carla Sofia Ferreira**, poet and teacher, author of *Ironbound Fados (Ghost City Press, 2019)*

Contents

I.

II.

For Daniel, Emily, and Elizabeth

I.

HALF-HEARTED

you say I look like an afternoon. like a Tuesday.
like a sad daydreamy flower girl when I want to look
like I can bite off fingers. I think my fatal flaw is
I never apologize for the things I say when my
aries moon takes over because I mean it. but everyone
knows I mean it— that's why it does so much damage.
my metal whip mouth. my shrapnel mouth. have you ever
cried in public, silent and raw-faced and fenced in by
strangers, but everyone avoids your eyes and says nothing
because you wear the kind of grief that makes people
uncomfortable? I have, far too many times. I am an expert
at crying in public but that doesn't make it any easier to
swallow that bitter peach pit of shame. it always knocks
into organs on its way down, like, *I'm here, knock knock.*
I live in you now, knock knock. the easiest way to describe
my current mental state is the time we visited wellton,
arizona when a dust storm came strolling in and there
was nowhere to run, so we crumpled down with arms
over heads and I never thought to be afraid of leaves but
they left white-hot scrape-kisses all over my skin. the truth
is there are ghosts with hands in my mouth. the truth is
they sound a lot like machine lovers squealing into my teeth.
this summer sucked the life out of me so slowly, so
unwillingly, like a car repossession. like it was almost sorry.
keep your doors open and your expectations abysmal and
you'll never cry yourself to sleep again. there was a bird
with a broken neck in my driveway and it made me think
of you. there was a dead cat splayed on the 101 and it made
me think of you. I hope you take this as a compliment. I want
you to tell me how you're feeling. I want you to mean it.
I care, Daniel. I promise.

SUNLIGHT MASSACRE

after Zoe Canner

you're surviving only on gummy vitamins now / five-day-old water / swiped hunks of bread from the kitchen in early morning / you nibble at it by breaking off the softest parts / rolling them into a ball / savoring them quietly / hardened crumbs keep you company in bed / tiny stabs at exposed flesh / the occasional bowl of cinnamon toast crunch at 4am / when the hunger has finally drowned out the whine of the city / you sip the milk left over for hours / tinged sweet but not quite enough to quench your thirst / cold creeps in through the bottom of your feet / up your shins / decidedly anchors into your kneecaps / your room is a mountain range & an avalanche / an uncharted sea & the brain-crushing pressure at the bottom of it / an early graveyard / but most of all it isn't yours / not the pillows stained with mascara & twin drops of blood / not the broken dresser drawers / nor the giant spider spiraling slow on your ceiling / you never learned how to keep a space clean if you never loved it / if you never loved yourself / you only know how to wade deeper into bedsheets / and sunlight massacres / you are made of chipped nail polish and sore, squeezed eyelids and not enough answers / never enough answers

WE'RE ALL SAD HERE

my brother is just as sad as I am. at night,
he smokes the moon out in the backyard. it's
a miracle— the way he rolls it so perfectly,
so delicately between his fingertips.
my brother is more angry-sad— meaning
his sadness catches fire because it can't find
any other way out. sometimes he sits in traffic,
just screaming from some deep, wounded
place inside him, spit flying through his
windshield like rust-tinted hail. I'm angry-sad
too, sometimes, but only at my father and
my abuser and trump. otherwise, I'm just
sad-sad. it paints my retinas blue and crushes
poison ivy leaves into my lemonade. I cough
up the sharpest safety pins and the brightest
feathers. in a restaurant, my mother laughs
at the way my brother and I share the same
rain cloud, as if she doesn't still hide her
kitchen knives. my brother tells me he hates
that bitch serotonin, the way she perpetually
leaves him drunk and scooped empty. I still
consider sneaking some lexapro into his
chicken parmesan. but this is a funk. a
sprawling barren state. we're all learning to
be sad and alive at the same time. to pull
the hurting thing from our chests without
making everybody uncomfortable. I sing
my sad into my salad, and it tells me there's
something glittering on the other side of this.
my brother calmly turns to the waitress
and tells her he wants to die.

EVERYTHING I OWN IS COVERED IN YELLOW HAIR

and I don't know where it came from or what to make of it. strands
of sunflower, mac 'n' cheese yellow make homes in my pillow, in
the ripped sleeve of my sweater, in the furrows of my brain. they say
in an emergency, a crayon will burn for half an hour. imagine: thirty
minutes of firetruck-red panic, pools of white-hot cerulean in piles at
your feet. imagine the kind of desperation it must have taken to start
lighting everything around you on fire and hope it somehow saves you.
I'm finding every minute is a new emergency, new punching dreams
and lung screams. I'm moving through today as if this isn't all half-
assed motions, as if my mind isn't still in weeks ago and the rest of me
is begging it to catch up. my brain is pumpkin guts. my brain is a
ledge-jumper, a time traveler. my brain catches the day flickering on and
off every time the sun winks. it's night now, and an ambulance is crawling
back home, its steady, somber headlights sighing, *we didn't make it in time,*
and I'm stumbling back from the window, hurt that I could catch the
world in a moment of such heartsick intimacy. it's two weeks ago and the
thing I spit up is rust-colored and tongue-numbing. the pills aren't working.
the out-of-order sign was lost in the uproar. I'm sitting numb in time's
soundwaves and every somersaulting minute is a new emergency.
everything I own is covered in yellow hair, and I'm lighting every strand
on fire in hopes you smell the smoke and shiver.

HOW TO TELL A DREAM FROM REALITY

are there starfish in the sky again?
is venus oozing slow, its sneezes
the color of white wine? when you
think of blood, do other people's
dogs sigh? can you speak to your
father? are you screaming again?
trace your fate line with the glass
wing of a beetle. if it hurts, cut it
off. if it bleeds, remember your
father. when she lays her head on
your lap, do her eyes flutter open
this time, her hands shaped like
constellations? or does her mouth
gape open with worms? is her neck
hanging limp at your touch? are
you screaming again? are there
green feathers covering the moon?
does the sound of shovels hitting
skulls make you feel like a child
again? she's looking up at you. her
lips caught around the word, *hurry.*

THE POET'S HOUSE AT 7AM

my sister smooths a jumper over her polo
shirt. it is green and plaid and freshly pressed
and her little fingers shiver from cold. she can't
get the zipper up, thinks of asking my mother
for help, decides against it. she leaves the zipper
down, her bedroom flutters with a pink glow.
someone downstairs is filling a bottle with water,
the sloshes echoing all through the house. my father
sleeps. my dog lies on the couch facing the window,
watching stray cars drive past. she's not supposed
to be on the furniture, and she knows this, but she
does it anyway because who else will watch
the windows? the doors? the people here trail in
and out, looking at the floor or cursing the sky.
my mother is awake, my grandmother gently
snoring beside her. my mother is awake but she
doesn't want to be. she tries to lie down for
another minute. absorb the day. swallow the bitter
rage bubbling under every slice of her skin.
she decides she's wasting precious time, storms
out of the room with that fury still swimming in
her mouth. my father sleeps, alone in that brooding
room, that california king-sized mattress. someone
downstairs is tentatively opening the back door.
they smoke a penultimate cigarette, listen to
the birds screeching hymns at the sun. I have
been awake for hours. my eyes become people
and those people are screaming. I bathe in
early morning silence, no sound but the city
stretching its jaws in a yawn. and when the house
wakes up, it anxiously tucks me into bed. but I am

sitting by the railings like I did as a child, ingesting
all the howls that escaped from the living room.
I am in the kitchen cutting my sister's sandwiches
the way she likes them. I am on the staircase
making music with the steps that creak. I am in
the walls and in the air ducts and in the sewers.
I am under the carpet and at the bottom of
the swimming pool. there is whispering, car doors
opening and slamming shut, and every sound
chimes against my flesh. my sister is crying
on her way to school. my father sleeps.

SALVIA

my potted plant deserves a better mother.
she wakes to strawberry-stained light and
my heart splattered all over the walls. she
teaches herself to sip moisture from the air,
crisp and cold as long-buried bone. she
watches my face drift in and out of waking
and says, *this girl must be the child of unraveled
grief and soft-edged intentions.* if I was a hand,
I'd be a child palm scraped bloody from
asphalt. if I was an animal, I'd be a firefly
sizzled in blackened forest lung. if I was an
expression of love, I'd be the flowers left
behind for a ghost. if I was birdsong, I'd be
one unholy, unending scream. my potted
plant smells of warm moonlight even when
her leaves wither. she packs resilience into
tiny boxes living unaware inside her. I give
her all the water in my blood. we eat sunlight
like it's a dying meal.

MOUNTAIN DEW

my mind has floated away from my body,
hovering at the ceiling like a freshly
murdered ghost girl. my roommates'
voices overlap, dance circles around
my holographic ears, more sound than
sentences. when I leave, they'll wonder
what drugs I must be on. I trudge out
in the cold in a t-shirt and skirt because
my skin needs to remember there's
still time. the cold does nothing to tether
my head back to my throat. my body
is flickering, more off than on. at
the supermarket at the corner, I reach
for one of those pudding cups I used to
love as a little girl and my hands pick up
an 8-pack of mountain dew several
aisles away. [*what am I wearing again?*
would my corpse be identifiable?] I stagger
across an unfamiliar grass field dragging
more food than I can afford, more than
I have room for [*subconsciously, I am*
stockpiling for the end of the world.] every
time my brain shivers, I can't tell where
I am. either it's snowing in phoenix
or the stars are finally scattering seeds
into my hair. my mind is floating away
from my body, but it will resurface in
a few days, concerned at the new cuts
and bruises strewn all over my hands.
in my dreams, I beg myself not to wake up.

INHALE / EXHALE

I wake up to the sound of my brother bleating like a pig / my sister gulping grief right behind him / I'm trying to sleep through the afternoon / wake up to quieter suffering / when the moon ate the sun, my siblings only saw / the lonesomeness dancing circles around the two / while I watched flower petals bow themselves / into crescent-shaped fingernails / look at these rooms / all the memories they hold / white walls painted over by yellow that absorbed too much light / always knew it was trying too hard / these door hinges have seen god / the stain above the bed frame / doesn't want to know what birthed it / there's no mirrors in this house / we just have to trust there's no more blood / nothing trickling from our sides / my brother holds steering wheels like dandelion-blown death wishes / he says existing is courageous / but right now, he feels like a coward / I say / *you're heroic just for not screaming* / I say / *you can exhale now* / *I promise* / sister, if you need me, please scream / brother, I pray this isn't the last time I see you / in the light snaking from the crack in your door in the middle of the night / in the car disappearing quiet around the corner.

PERSONALITY QUIZ

if your soul was an ice cream, what flavor would it be?
- a. rainbow sherbet melting peach-pink on your father's child-fingers.
- b. rocky road but instead of nuts there are the beaks of baby doves. the marshmallows are already on fire.
- c. something purple and star-dusted that swivels like the head of an owl and eats the tongues of men with hats.
- d. a pile of dirty snow and wisdom teeth.

if you were to rip the skin from your chest, what color would the yarn be underneath?
- a. winter's sighs.
- b. green like mermaid's sharpest canines.
- c. your father's grief, unburied.
- d. her fingernails the night you dove into the street.

in a past life, you:
- a. were a world-renowned figure skater, murdered by the blade of your own skates.
- b. removed the safety pins holding together your ribs, laid back and let the dust take you.
- c. watched the salt water eat your arms bony and bare and water-speckled. you used to hate the beach when you were young. today, it tells you things you can't understand.
- d. held her a little closer before the elevator doors shut. before the pushpins on bedspreads, the unanswered cries for help.

if you stand still long enough:
- a. the trees speak their own language, and you just begin to understand it.

b.   she comes back, spins around twice, won't look you in the eye.

c.   you should have loved her louder (*you don't know*)

d.   your elbows become the windows to your soul (*those crooked, sharp things, all the black eyes they've birthed*)

with what kind of wine would you be paired?

a.   something too sweet, that sizzles against your lungs (*forgiveness is a screaming thing*)

b.   something haloed by the sound of vomit, early morning (*just let me have this*)

c.   something pale, like her skin as she tried to stumble home (*please*)

d.   something that nestles you like shark-toothed velvet. something that won't let you forget.

POEM FOR WINTER

once, in the dead of winter, a dog pushes
my brother into the pool. I am six and I
watch him flounder and sink until my
mother runs screaming to drag him out.
once, in the dead of winter, I teach myself
to do a scratch spin on a small, muddy
patch of ice in the middle of downtown
phoenix. there are dozens of people around
me, shrieking and stumbling and gathering
fake snow in red hands. I spin so fast, the city
goes quiet for one sliver-sized second. I spin
so fast, the world flickers and shuts off.
once, I wake up to this state's shivering,
the heat sunk back to hell with its tail tucked
between its legs. my phone tells me it's
barely 60 degrees, but my fingers and toes
wail louder and wither like old grapes, like
anniversary flowers. I want winter to feel
more like a hallmark movie, like frosted
windows and unattended fires and my house
asphyxiating in snow. I want hot chocolate
pouring sweet and scalding down my
desert-parched throat. I want to rub these
tender tongue-burns against the roof of my
mouth for days. once, in the dead of winter,
I wrap my body in christmas lights and sit
in a dark room to get into the holiday spirit,
until each color sears itself into my brain, until
red and green smoke wanders out of my ears.
I blink at the lights and they blink back at me
to the tune of a death march.

THESE DAYS, I ONLY GET TEXTS FROM MY PHARMACY, BEGGING ME TO PICK UP MY PRESCRIPTIONS

I wish my pharmacy was proud to have my antidepressants
the way they unabashedly announce they carry viagra.
the man in front of me in line smugly shells out $15
to make his dick hard, and yet the pharmacist pulls me
aside to whisper that if I feel like killing myself again,
please call. she hands me the discreet paper bag of my
salvation, says, *here's your lung-saver / your blood-warmer.*
here's what makes living just a little more bearable, but please,
be quiet / be ashamed about it.

also

that'll be $600.

POEM FOR EFFEXOR

three weeks of you / and my skin smiles from
another girl's face / I'm melting / I'm flooding /
one twitch-footed decision after another / I'm
falling in love with curly-haired girls / and boys
who rub the melancholy / from my brain / I fall
in love self-destructively / singing invincibility fables
from bullet-shredded hands / you're pouring down
my throat / you're swimming in my blood / swelling
until my veins burst / I'm all crystalline and eager
hand shakes / biting clavicles like soft-sinewed
lifelines / tasting and tasting your endless orange /
hint of sweet in all this numb / hint of living in all
this gray / I'm dancing in ice-bathed parking lots /
molding my breaths into flowers for airplanes /
screaming *I'm alive I'm alive I'm alive I'm alive*

II.

EMERGENCY BREAK

my brother threatens to drive us into a wall again,
his rage as tangible as burnt metal scraps flying
across asphalt, another red light and he's seeing
red. we could've been siamese twins once,
connected by one furiously screaming heart. two
wild heads, two bodies splayed spider-like from
the ribs. I had to slice myself away to survive, let
him keep my half because he needed it much more
than I did. he's become so many things I am terrified of
and I want to tell him there's life beneath his anger,
peaking green out at the carnage. a whole person
babbling newborn outside his hurt, waiting to become
him. I want to tell him, *I want to love you but you
make it so impossible. I want to dull your edges but
I keep cutting myself and I'm almost bled dry.* all his
weight's on the gas, he doesn't know his way around
the brakes or the words *I'm sorry.* he only knows how
to spew venom and curse god, lives like his one
purpose is to let death engulf him in flames. but I
will throw myself from this vehicle, ash-covered and
grief-shaken. I won't look back at the wreckage. and
I will teach myself to stop feeling guilty about it.

SCENES FROM AN ISLAND

I built this tiny speck of land.
[it takes the form of my heart,
reshapes itself after every
disappointment.] I built the sea
that huddles ever-closer, and
the coral reef skyscrapers
in that sea. I built the volcano
that spews juniper berries in
the night, both soundless and
screaming. I suppose, at the end
of every day— and every slow-
aching life nestled in between
them— I am an inherently selfish
creature. all the messages in
every tear-filled bottle read,
where did you go? and *we love you so—*
even with the fishhooks we stuck
in your back. my island flinches,
inches further and further away.
somedays, the sun flits dancing
through the trees like a blue-
winged memory. I make a bed
on the beach, watch you drown
through binoculars. I bury myself
in the sand, in the hope that I can
finally escape your howls.

SETTLING IN

I'm settling knee-deep into the fact
that I am trying my absolute hardest.
I'm giving it my all, my best, and it's
not nearly enough. My best looks like
lazy, like *irresponsible*, like *fickle* and
distant and *selfish* and *ungrateful*.
I'm letting so many things slip under
the table. I'm marinating in
the disappointment of everyone I love
and there's so much of it. I'm skinning
myself, bleeding myself dry, white-flagged
and hanging on a clothesline. there's
still so much I need to do, so much
I've yet to be. and I just hang. I float,
useless in the hot breeze.

SELF-PORTRAIT COVERED IN MOLASSES

there's a coral reef in my bedroom,
sharp things flying in through the window.
my hair the mousetrap and the gutters,
my skin tries to remember how to be skin.
I ache. I lung. I wormhole. I hold yesterday
in the minutes between my fingers,
the grape juice between my synapses.
I am warpath burning slow to the bone.
crawl my face back onto this skull, eyes
dipped in gasoline. you say I was supposed
to leave half an hour ago. you stretch
hurry into eight syllables and I remind
myself to be impressed tomorrow. I remind
myself of jewel beetle legs and girls in
bicycle lanes and moons made of balled-up
taco bell napkins. I burst into rooms like
a half-drowned toddler and everyone
is staring. I say *don't worry these eyebags
are prada* and stuff all my clocks inside.
the minute hand sneezes six times in a row
and no one says bless you. the hour hand
has fallen in love with the sun.

JULY MONEY

I don't know how to tell you this,
but your son is breaking again. a self-
burial. he's getting high again, crouching
in a room without light bulbs and wishing
he could see outside the gloom in his own
skull. I always see him when I sleep,
shrinking paler and thinner, his eyes wild
and dead and roadkilled. today I reminded
him he has a future, and he just shrugged
and asked for more money. and I wanted to
shake him, wanted to ask how he managed
such a disappearing act. wanted to tell him,
*you're supposed to be my big brother. I was supposed
to resent you forever.* I don't know how to tell you
this, because I shouldn't be the only one noticing,
watching, prodding his skin. I don't know how
to leave my own brother for dead, or how to fill
his shoes. I don't know how to be your golden
child. I'm all flinches and face-punch daydreams.
you say, *we're so proud of you.* you say, *look at you,
graduating college, making it look easy.* look at me,
dragging myself to class, skinned-bloody knees,
avoiding the gaze of my classmates. look at me,
slipping through storm drains under crowded feet.
still mapping my own death like it's the event
of the century. my brother once asked me,
*what gene do we carry that makes it so hard to function
like regular people?* and I tried to laugh, tried to
believe he wasn't making a good point. I don't
know how to tell you this, but sometimes when I
text him and don't hear back for days, I think

to myself, *my brother is dead. he's hung himself in a dark and dusty room, and no one has noticed yet*, until he gets the nerve to text back. it's not a sad, frightening, or desperate thought. it just sits there, ghostly and blooming, cold and sharp and matter-of-fact.

WOOZY

kiss me Mr. Cyclops:
I'm drifting away half-dead anyway,
fingers stained forever with scarlet.
not blood, I promise, though I hate how
I wipe and wipe my hands and it never comes off.
I'm no mess, I tell you, I'm a scream half-loose,
blind and sore, but just new, you see:
I was born right here, my eyes bleeding fire and fury.
listen, you can't just throw the blame at everyone.
so the tides turned against you,
so everyone you know is dying, so what?
I think you don't play fair because that means
someone is always losing, and this time it doesn't have to be you.
Mr. Cyclops, you're due for a smile;
your one eye has looked so weary for far too long.
consume me whole, swallowed down and buttered up.
that might turn us both around, wouldn't it?
maybe then my mother will take a better look
and she'll grab my shoulders and say *what has he—*
what has he done— what has he been doing to you?

MIRACLE DRUG

I'm on the hunt for a miracle drug // one I'm becoming
increasingly sure doesn't actually exist // I am a prozac
trainwreck // a lexapro jitterbug // wellbutrin's
morning spit-up and trazodone's bloodshot eyes //
effexor drips unsure from my system // and my brother
wants to know which antidepressant // won't make him
want to die // any more than he already does // and
I am not a liar // I'm just silent // a girl on the news
worships a helmet // that electrocutes her into
euthymia // my mother begs *please, let's try* // but I'm so
tired of trying // tired of co-leasing this body // tired of
being guinea-pigged so my siblings don't have to ache //
quite this badly // I say *I hurt, Mama, I hurt* // no,
my miracle drug doesn't exist // I wouldn't even know
what I'm tasting if my lips touched it // wouldn't even
remember which neurotransmitters I'm waiting to hear
back from // should this melancholia quit me in the middle
of the night // would I even notice? // *I'm scared Mama* //
I'm so fucking scared and small // I don't remember what it's like
to not be depressed // and she strokes my hair for
the first time in years // and she says //
one day you won't remember a single thing.

POEM FOR THE THINGS THAT TRIGGER ME

1. the toilet flushing
    that blast like a bomb bursting the morning stillness
2. the buzz of my phone
    endless and angry like a scorned bee
    and all the people caring enough to check in on me
3. tall, aggressively confident straight men
    and how I know I couldn't fight back
    how I shrink
    and forget how to speak
4. the sensation of metal
    scraping against metal
5. the way I can wrap my fingers around your forearm
    effortlessly
6. the moon,
    hanging swollen above me, close enough to breathe
    like the pockmarked face of a martyr
7. the screeching
    the clawing
    pin-pricking across my skull
    nails dragging against my brain
8. your ribs peeking out, frightened
    from canvas-stretched skin
9. certain five-letter names
10. news stories of women who fought back
    and still didn't make it
11. an intersection downtown
    the sun crouching low behind skyscrapers
    the restaurant on the northwest corner
    faces peering from third-floor apartment windows
12. the way you give this illness a name
    mold her into a girl in your head

the way you call her a friend
while she stares at you greedily
13. the pictures I stumble upon at 15
the hip bones
the chins carved from jagged glass
you tell me *this is what god looks like*
I've gone cold but I force myself to keep looking
I'm sick
we're so sick
14. a french movie, bathed in red
and I can't stop shaking for hours after
and I hurt because she hurts
15. and you, looking over your shoulder one last time
don't worry about me, still playful
still skirting the line between girl and ghost
your skin is gray, you haven't bled in seasons
you're slipping from my fingers and I don't know who to call
16. I didn't hear you were dead until months later

APOLOGY TOUR

I tell my mother I can no longer brush my hair,
the tangle-tugging makes the zaps in my brain
far too loud. I sit wailing on the kitchen floor
like a child, and my hair is exploding in clumps
above my head, and my body aches from
how hard it works just to keep myself awake,
and I want so badly just to die. my mother runs
to get her hairbrush and sweetly runs it through
my head as if I were a child. I want to tell her not to
bother. I swallow the pain the way it swallows me,
over and over ad infinitum, an ouroboros of hurt
droning like the tired bees in my head. she wants
so badly to feel like she can do something, so
I say nothing. she undoes all the knots from
my hair, and the neighborhood cats knead
the broken bricks from my back, and the pigeons
trim the stray threads from my clothes. I am soft
and useless like a child, and I want to die like a child,
scattered in cracked riverbeds. my mother says
it will all be over soon, she sees the end just
beyond this last snarl. by now I know there is no
end, just me shrinking and rising and falling,
capsizing and fighting for footing, making my
apology tour around the world when I can finally
stand. *I'm sorry,* I cry out to booing crowds. *I'm so
sorry it's been months since I've spoken to you. I'm
sorry I disappeared without warning, without a smoke
signal. I'm so sorry, I haven't been well, I'm afraid.
I'm sorry. I still love you. I'm sorry. I haven't been well.
I'm not well. I'm not well. I'm not well. I'm not well.*

SELF PORTRAIT AS BIRD FLYING INTO A WINDOW

and when you pull over, you're still screaming,
hands held shaking in front of you like the skin

of them must not be real. my body hurled into
your windshield like mid-autumn hailstorm. my body

leaves streaks of blood and feathers and blindsided
desecration. my body the railroad tracks and

the trainwreck. the punching bag and the percussion
instrument. the pigeon queen, at once both sickness

and softness. you're stumbling out of your vehicle,
sobs chiming from your throat. you see from

far away a mash of gray and white and red and bone.
tell yourself you can look at me up close. the carnage,

and the tenderness vomited from its mouth. there is
a strange grief inside you and you don't know how

to free it from your ribs. there was a grief inside me,
and it spills an ocean on this asphalt.

HOW TO TELL A DREAM FROM REALITY
(REPRISE)

are you spiraling? have you been
spiraling this whole time, unnoticed
and cornered all at once? are you
letting that man eat you out again
in the parking lot of a shopping
mall? so mature of you. you move
so jerky, little marionette girl. are
those mirtazapine tablets falling out
of your mouth, or rotten teeth? did
you kill her? you did, didn't you?
just once, or a dozen times? how
many times did you have to beat her
down before she stopped standing
up, before she stopped wailing *please*?
you tear a hole in the screen of her
parents' bedroom window when she
finally lies still. you tumble through
the night like a snowball, gaining
speed but not substance. tell me,
are you dead yet? the effexor tried
to kill you just like all the others.
it is no longer in your body and
you feel its useless absence. you
keep taking it so your body doesn't
miss it, so those *missing-you* symptoms
don't finally destroy you. your mind
is no longer in your body. your
heartbeat is no longer in your body.
it is in the walls. you are tracing

the cracks with shaking fingers. you
are palpitating. is this your life, the
one you're living? are you anyone's
hero? you text your boyfriend
sometime during intermission though
you can't quite remember opening
your eyes. your hands are made of eels.
something sits heavy on your chest.
you're crying for help, you're
remembering even clouds weigh
many tons. you remember you are
nothing and it doesn't stop hurting.
you're screaming like the child in you
did not quite die when you thought
she did. you are emaciated. you don't
know what it's like to not want to die.
you are jumping out of 12th story
windows and resurfacing somewhere
at the very beginning. and you punch
yourself in the face without warning,
your mother startles so badly she
drops a whole bag of flour on the floor,
staring at you with mouth agape. *I want
to wake up* you say weakly. you can't stop
punching yourself, can't stop screaming
I want to wake up. your mother is sobbing.
from 700 miles away, your brother's
hellmouth splits in fifths and shrieks
you're more awake than you've been in months.
your little sister walks into the kitchen
and sets herself on fire.

TO-DO LIST

- wake up.
- take your pills with the half-empty mountain dew in your fridge. the fizz has gone. you can't taste it anyway.
- think of the first thing you'll do as a ghost while you mess up your eyeshadow.
- tell yourself to move faster. the clocks have grown tired of waiting for you. everyone you pass can see your mess. everyone you know is perpetually disappointed in you.
- don't think of your family.
- don't think of your family.
- remind yourself to eat something today.
- paint *I'm okay* onto your tongue, practice saying it every time you breathe. it takes shape, hollow and neon blue in the air. eyebrows knit together. *I'm not okay*, you try again. *but I'm trying.*
- cry in another public bathroom stall. play sudoku on your phone because it distracts your brain from the ache. call a friend and cut yourself off on the first ring. hide for the next hour, until the sobs stop coming. you're glad for the mirrors, for your sunglasses. for the hand soap that smells vaguely of roses and dreaming.
- tell yourself to get something to eat.
- don't think of your family.
- don't think of the people you left behind, the ones you couldn't save. the little girl you deserted in the house of leather belts. the dogs gasping for air in the middle of the night.
- dance circles around face-fallen explanations. *I'm not lazy, not selfish. I just can't move.* dance circles until they sound more like excuses.
- ~~tell yourself~~ ask yourself nicely to eat.
- tear up every time a stranger looks you in the eye. whisper apologies to no one.
- fall asleep, twitching and fighting through decade-long dreams. sleep until you can't recognize the time of year.

- call a friend and sit face to face with their voicemail inbox. your tongue has given up. the sun has given up.
- don't think of your family.
- don't imagine your brother dying. a hundred times, in a hundred different ways. the same song at the same funeral. don't imagine your brother's body. his pale hands forever making fists like he fought god on his way out.
- *eat please just fucking eat.*
- think of what you'll do as a ghost. like replace the flowers in your mother's vase every time they droop. like write poems on bathroom walls for the next crying girl. like fly into the sun and lace stars into your veins.
- build a home out of your own grief. there's horse-sized fish swimming in the walls, holes in the roof. the ground is littered with broken, colored glass.
- sleep only when the light peeks in through half-covered eyelids.
- wake up.
- *wake up.*
- please.

NOON

I turn around, towards the window. if tomorrow never comes, whose mouth did I tumble into, swished around and spit out? does it matter? I wake up alone at the end of the world, contact lenses gorilla-glued to my eyes, mascara oozing down one half-melted cheek. the sticky notes on my bedpost say I forgot to take my pills, forgot to call my mother, forgot to feed my fires. the tango in my brain deafeningly agrees. they also say, a little softer, *your body is not a rehab center,* and I pull the glass doors closer to me. I compress. the floor of my ribcage grows dusty and I forget what else I have to offer. I realize no one has ever taken me out dancing and it's all my fault. but I'm trying to be kinder to my past self. my non-existent future self. all my idiot selves. I breathe in ash. it is springtime on the moon again. I dreamt I had red hair again. I dreamt of couch fires and writing the same prayer three thousand times. I dreamt she had more time, and god had more teeth. in the graying light, my skin looks moth-kissed, dew-foraged. I leave the birds rotting in my hair. when the sun bleeds out, I'll try again.

we'll try again, Daniel.

LUNA MOTH

sometimes I still make eyes at
oncoming traffic, but I hold my head above
the waves. I swallow my pills dry, accept
that this heart is thrumming now, though
I never asked it to, that one day it will
be forty and float lighter in my ribcage.
I picture it: crawling out of a chrysalis,
shiny green and crumpled. I will do
my own taxes, pick out my own furniture.
Liz is gentler, softer in my dreams.
no longer screaming the suicide hotline
number in my face, telling me she could've
been found still warm-blooded. she presses
her cheek against mine, her thigh against
my thigh. one skeletal, one wide and
muscular at last. my brother throws his pills
into the sea and finally comes home.

Acknowledgments

"half-hearted" : *Rabid Oak.*

"we're all sad here" and "miracle drug" : *Peculiars Magazine*

"EVERYTHING I OWN IS COVERED IN YELLOW HAIR" :
Philosophical Idiot.

"how to tell a dream from reality" : *Minute Magazine.*

"the poet's house at 7 am" : *Drunk Monkeys.*

"salvia" : *Dirty Paws Poetry* & *Lux Undergraduate Creative Review.*

"mountain dew" and "emergency break" : *Crepe & Penn.*

"inhale / exhale" : *The Hellebore Press.*

"personality quiz" : *Terse Journal.*

"poem for winter" : *Marias at Sampaguitas.*

"woozy" : *Dodging the Rain.*

"poem for the things that trigger me" : *The Confessionalist Zine.*

"self-portrait as bird flying into a window" : *South Broadway Ghost Society.*

"to-do list" : *Ghost City Review.*

Wanda Deglane is a night-blooming desert flower from Arizona. She is the daughter of Peruvian immigrants and a recent graduate of Arizona State University, where she will also pursue a master's degree in Marriage and Family Therapy. Her poetry has been published or forthcoming from *Glass Poetry, Cosmonauts Avenue, Yes Poetry,* and elsewhere. Wanda is the author of *Rainlily* (2018), *Honey-Laced Garbage Dreams* (Ghost City Press, 2019), *Bittersweet* (Vegetarian Alcoholic Press, 2019), *passionfruit* (2020), *Venus in Bloom* (Porkbelly Press, 2020), and *penumbra* (Ghost City Press, 2020).

CPSIA information can be obtained
at www.ICGtesting.com
Printed in the USA
BVHW071017070521
606655BV00008B/1561